BBC MUSIC GUIDES

SCHUMANN ORCHESTRAL MUSIC

BBC MUSIC GUIDES

Bach Cantatas J. A. WESTRUP
Bach Organ Music PETER WILLIAMS
Bartók Orchestral Music JOHN MC CABE
Beethoven Concertos and Overtures ROGER FISKE
Beethoven Piano Sonatas DENIS MATTHEWS
Beethoven String Quartets BASIL LAM
Beethoven Symphonies ROBERT SIMPSON
Berlioz Orchestral Music HUGH MACDONALD
Brahms Chamber Music IVOR KEYS
Brahms Piano Music DENIS MATTHEWS
Brahms Orchestral Music JOHN HORTON
Brahms Songs ERIC SAMS
Bruckner Symphonies PHILIP BARFORD
Debussy Orchestral Music DAVID COX
Debussy Piano Music FRANK DAWES
Dvořák Symphonies and Concertos ROBERT LAYTON
Elgar Orchestral Music MICHAEL KENNEDY
Handel Concertos STANLEY SADIE
Haydn String Quartets ROSEMARY HUGHES
Haydn Symphonies H. C. ROBBINS LANDON
Mahler Symphonies and Songs PHILIP BARFORD
Mendelssohn Chamber Music JOHN HORTON
Monteverdi Madrigals DENIS ARNOLD
Mozart Chamber Music A. HYATT KING
Mozart Piano Concertos PHILIP RADCLIFFE
Mozart Wind and String Concertos A. HYATT KING
Rachmaninov Orchestral Music PATRICK PIGGOTT
Ravel Orchestral Music LAURENCE DAVIES
Schoenberg Chamber Music ARNOLD WHITTALL
Schubert Chamber Music J. A. WESTRUP
Schubert Piano Sonatas PHILIP RADCLIFFE
Schubert Songs MAURICE J. E. BROWN
Schubert Symphonies MAURICE J. E. BROWN
Schumann Piano Music JOAN CHISSELL
Schumann Songs ASTRA DESMOND
Shostakovich Symphonies HUGH OTTAWAY
Tchaikovsky Ballet Music JOHN WARRACK
Tchaikovsky Symphonies and Concertos JOHN WARRACK
The Trio Sonata CHRISTOPHER HOGWOOD
Vaughan Williams Symphonies HUGH OTTAWAY
Vivaldi MICHAEL TALBOT

BBC MUSIC GUIDES

Schumann Orchestral Music

HANS GAL

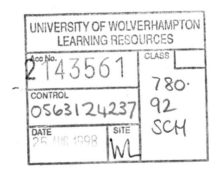
BRITISH BROADCASTING CORPORATION

Contents

Introduction   5

The Symphonies   12

The Overtures   37

The Concertos   49

Published by the
British Broadcasting Corporation
35 Marylebone High Street
London W1M 4AA

ISBN 0 563 12423 7

First published 1979

Typeset in Great Britain by Eta Services (Typesetters) Ltd., Beccles, Suffolk
Printed in England by Whitstable Litho Ltd., Whitstable, Kent

Introduction

A period of supreme achievement leaves to its successors a rich heritage, but also peculiar and difficult problems. Music after Beethoven offers an abundance of illustrations of this point. When Robert Schumann was born – 8 June 1810 – Beethoven was at the apex of his creative activity; and there was no musician of Schumann's generation in Germany who did not worship Beethoven and his work. The history of instrumental music in the nineteenth century could be condensed into an analysis of the different ways in which Beethoven's heritage was interpreted by his followers. Schubert, Mendelssohn and Schumann, Berlioz and Wagner, Chopin, Brahms and Bruckner – they all had to find their individual solutions, their individual answers to the problem, and each of them, in his individual way, contributed to the complexity of music in the nineteenth century.

It is not always easy to distinguish between organic, authentic developments and spurious trends, between style and fashion; and there is no doubt that the latter has assumed an ever-increasing power through publicity since, in the course of the 1820s, journalism, for good or ill, became an ever stronger influence in the intellectual world. Robert Schumann was the first great musician to take up the challenge, the first to set out to defend what he regarded as noble and genuine artistic efforts against questionable, spurious currents by founding his own publication, the *Leipzig Neue Zeitschrift für Musik*, whose editor he remained for ten years. Much as for us today Schumann's literary and publicistic contributions seem mainly of historical interest, it is true that Schumann the courageous critic and imaginative writer became known sooner than Schumann the composer. His fictitious double character of Florestan and Eusebius – the fierce and the mild critic – and his slogan of 'The war of the League of David against the Philistines' are known to every piano player from some of Schumann's finest piano works. His most outstanding merit as a critic was his uncanny instinct for discovering genius from its very first manifestations, as he did in the cases of Chopin, Berlioz and Brahms.

With music, the distance of a century offers a reasonably reliable test of durability. Among Schumann's orchestral works his symphonies and his Piano Concerto have stood this test with an ever youthful vigour, and as a piano composer, a songwriter and a composer of chamber music – chiefly with his Piano Quintet, his Piano Quartet and String Quartets – he has always remained in the repertoire. It is true that this durability does not by any means extend to the whole of his very extensive oeuvre, and there are reasons for this. But the measure of an artist's achievement must certainly be taken from the very best of his output. No truly great work has ever been written by anyone who was not a great composer; but there are inferior works by the great, and some even by the greatest.

In this respect, however, the case of Schumann is peculiar because a most tragic circumstance is involved: he died at the age of forty-six after a total mental breakdown a couple of years before. The fatal illness from which he suffered, progressive paralysis of the brain,[1] tends to cast shadows on earlier years, and it certainly did so in Schumann's case. His awareness of the danger that threatened him is revealed in a letter to Clara Wieck (11 February 1838):

During the night of October 17, 1833, I suddenly had the most frightful thought a human being can possibly conceive – the most terrible that Heaven could inflict – that I might lose my reason. This thought took possession of me with such violence that all comfort, all prayer vanished as if it were idle mockery. This fear drove me from place to place – my breath stopped at the thought: 'What if you were no longer able to think?' Clara, anyone who has once been crushed like that knows no worse suffering, or illness, or despair, that could possibly happen to him.

It is not unlikely that Schumann's inclination to hectic, restless work at certain periods was at least partly due to an urge to concentrate all his mental powers in order to overcome a brooding, dismal feeling of physical and mental discomfort by the ecstasy of creating. Different characters react differently to stress and strain. Hugo Wolf, who suffered from the same affliction as Schumann, complains bitterly in his letters about periods of creative incapacity and enforced idleness. Schumann tried by heroic efforts to overcome such indisposition, and the result is a catastrophic list of casualties among the works of his later thirties and forties. He shared with Schubert a gift of the Gods which is not without certain dangers: glowing inspiration, coupled with an irresistible

---

[1] According to expert opinion, this is the only diagnosis consistent with Schumann's symptoms. (See Dr Eliot Slater and Dr Alfred Meyer in *Confinia Psychiatrica*, Vol. 2, No. 2, Basle–New York, 1959.)

urge to finish a work on the spur of the moment. Like Schubert he seems to have been disinclined to let an invention mature and grow into its proper shape by patient control. One will see the difference if one thinks of the creative habits of Schumann's greatest follower, Brahms, who kept some works that seemed problematic to him – his Piano Concerto in D minor and First Symphony are outstanding examples – on his desk for years before being able to finish them to his satisfaction. As for Schubert, the resulting problem is reflected in an amazing number of unfinished works, compositions that remained fragments owing to some temporary creative indisposition. Schumann's creative process seems to have been entirely governed by emotional factors, and this is one of the reasons for the irresistible emotional appeal of his music. On the other hand it was a permanent temptation to finish and even to publish works of questionable quality. There is no other great composer in whose music such a tremendous difference can be found between truly inspired work and what was written, as it were, *invita Minerva*, without the blessing of the Goddess, prone to move in certain habitual patterns of invention and lacking the spark of spontaneous inspiration. He would deceive himself by a frantic effort, but the result was treacherous. This kind of creative indisposition periodically affected the music Schumann wrote in his later years. Even in one of his most outstanding achievements, Scenes from Goethe's *Faust*, some parts, written at problematic periods, show the ominous fingerprints of his fate: stale episodes and an overture, written last, which lacks all the freshness of true Schumannian imagination. The same unfortunately applies to so many of his later songs, which cannot compare with the springtide of 1840 – the cycles *Myrthen, Dichterliebe, Liederkreis* and *Frauenliebe und Leben,* in which his immortality as a songwriter is anchored. Nor is there any comparison between his later piano music, even the poetically evocative *Waldscenen* and *Albumblätter*, and the magnificence of his early period, culminating in such works as *Novelletten, Fantasie, Etudes Symphoniques, Arabesque, Kinderscenen, Davidsbündler, Kreisleriana, Carnival* – one feels tempted to list all those precious twenty-eight works written during his twenties. We shall have to deal with this problem again with respect to his orchestral music.

There was another problem, that resulted from the comparatively late start of his professional training as a musician. He did not have the advantage of his predecessors such as Haydn, Mozart, Beethoven, Weber and Schubert of growing up in permanent contact with vocal and orchestral ensembles. Nor was he as fortunate as his close contemporary Mendelssohn, whose wealthy parents could afford everything necessary for the musical upbringing of an infant prodigy, even including an orchestra at home on Sunday mornings. Mendelssohn's Overture to *A Midsummer Night's Dream,* written when the composer was seventeen, and which he was never able to surpass as a masterpiece of composition and orchestration, drastically illustrates everything Schumann had to do without, stemming as he did from a middle-class family of scanty means and with a deeply rooted prejudice against a musical career with all its insecurity. Schumann, after wasting a couple of years with a desultory study of law, was twenty-one when he started serious studies of composition. 'My whole life', he had written to his mother one year before, 'has been twenty years of struggle between Poetry and Prose, or call it Music and Law'. In fact, Schumann was the first great composer who lacked the ability of a performer, and the first who had to acquire practical experience of the orchestra at a comparatively late stage of his career. During his studies in Leipzig he had the advantage of lessons from the best available piano teacher, Friedrich Wieck, whose daughter and pupil Clara became Schumann's wife. His own efforts at attaining pianistic virtuosity were frustrated by permanent damage to his right hand, incurred by violent methods of practising. All the same, his musical imagination remained rooted in the piano, and the first ten years of his creative activity were almost exclusively devoted to this instrument.

As regards its form, a piano piece by Schumann, with all its shapely melody, splendour of colour and brilliance of sound, is a conglomeration of small units in perfect balance. Contrast and recapitulation are all that is needed for a kind of construction in which the charm of the invention always maintains a spontaneous flow of events; and the recapitulations are nearly always exact repeats. Schumann had to arrive at a more spacious type of form when, in his thirties, he turned to orchestral and chamber music, with his First Symphony, his three string quartets and his Piano Quintet and Piano Quartet amongst his outstanding achievements. But here still, the constructive terseness of Beethoven was not within his reach. When he turns to the larger types of instrumental form, to sonata or rondo form, another predecessor looms much larger as his model: Franz Schubert, whom he adored with all his youthful enthusiasm at the time of his early beginnings and whose Great Symphony in C major he discovered on a visit to Vienna in 1838.

Schubert had always been his idol. Nine years earlier he had written to Friedrich Wieck:

Schubert is still 'my one and only Schubert', especially as he has everything in common with 'my one and only Jean Paul'; when I play Schubert it is like reading a novel by Jean Paul set to music. There is no music at all which is as psychologically remarkable in its progression and combination of ideas and its apparent leaps of logic as Schubert's. And how few have been able, as he was, to impress a single individuality on such a variety of tone pictures, and how few have written so much for themselves and for their own heart. Where others keep a diary to record their momentary feelings, etc., Schubert confided each of his passing moods to music paper, and his soul, musical through and through, wrote notes where others use words.

A catchword is a convenient label which can serve to give meaning to something otherwise elusive. The adjective 'romantic' is such a label, and it has been used and misused with respect to music for a century and a half. Romanticism (though its origins lie at least one generation back) had become fashionable in the 1820s and 1830s with lyrical poets such as Brentano, Eichendorff, Kleist and Rückert and extravagant writers like Jean Paul and E. T. A. Hoffmann in Germany, poets such as Byron, Shelley and Wordsworth in England, and Chateaubriand, Musset and Victor Hugo in France; and this fashion certainly had its specific influence on the young intellectuals of that period. As has happened so often in history, a younger generation was in open revolt against the restrictive discipline of its elders. Romantic influences are most obviously reflected in German opera, where for some decades anything other than a medieval subject was hardly acceptable. What young Schumann writes in his letters and diaries is very much coloured with the romantic idiom. He feels himself to be a poet, and he is inspired by poetry. He writes to a Frenchman, Simonin de Sire: '...Don't you know Jean Paul, our great writer? I have learnt more counterpoint from him than from any of my music teachers....'

It is hardly possible to give an exact definition of the stylistic attributes of romantic music, except for the rather negative feature of a common aversion to the transparent sound, emotional restraint and form-consciousness of classicism. The romantic is a lonely individual. He stands by himself, building a world of his own. This is why it is so difficult to identify consistent traits of romantic style which are applicable to a whole generation. An emphasis on imaginative and emotional elements in the conception of a work of art and an avoidance of constructive features of form is indeed all that remains in the end as a common feature of romanticism, in music as in poetry. As a fashion is always liable to exaggerations, indulgence in emotional extravagance plays a prominent part in the history of romanticism; but such an obviously striking feature should not be over-estimated. Individuals of this type may occasionally unite for a common purpose, but their real ends and aims will never coincide. This fact, and the abundance of brilliant individual talent, explains the extraordinary richness and variety of the romantic landscape, and the difficulty of defining it properly.

Right in the centre of this landscape stands young Schumann, the most consciously demonstrative follower of romantic ideals and fantasies. This is expressed in the great piano works of his twenties, in the effusiveness of the music as much as in certain oddities of added titles and remarks. It was only natural that his youthful extravagance had to cool down with his growing maturity.

Schumann's style is not easy to describe. Exuberance is certainly a most essential component of it, and a cool, detached approach to his music is as impossible for the listener as for the performer. His soul is in every expressive phrase he shapes, and the instrument has to sing it in order to do it justice. With all his urge for communication he is by nature an introvert. This is why his monologues at the piano, his own primary instrument, seem the most direct effluence of his soul, and why pianists will always love his music. The same directness has to inspire the performers of his orchestral music in order to reveal its truth. And a sophisticated rhythmical and harmonic structure inherent in his style demands a subtlety of shading, emphasising or softening certain parts of the texture, which requires an impeccable control of every detail, something that is not easily obtained, considering the usual *al fresco* manner of orchestral performing. Schumann demands the utmost perfection from his players; but he rewards it generously.

He seems to have been constitutionally unable ever to descend to any kind of banality, impressing a hallmark of distinction on everything he writes, be it music or prose. His secret is a subtlety of structure unequalled by any of his contemporaries. Even his seemingly plain, unassuming inventions create their tender appeal by means of hidden and sometimes very sophisticated harmonic or rhythmical details. One of Schumann's *Scenes from Childhood*, which is probably familiar to every music lover, will serve to demonstrate this: It is 'Träumerei' ('Day Dreaming'). In some respects this piece may be regarded as a model of simplicity: twenty-four bars, of which the first eight are repeated, grow from one four-bar phrase, and the harmonic range of the composition is limited to the tonic, the dominant and the subdominant. But what appears at first sight to be four bars in four-four time, is in fact an alternation of five-four, three-four and two-four bars, and if the player is not instinctively aware of this, if he puts clumsy bar accents on the opening note of every four-four bar, he will destroy all the intimate beauty of this lovely invention. Schumann's intention is made perfectly clear by a *crescendo* sign between the first and second bars as well as by the harmonic and rhythmical structure of the accompaniment and the phrasing, which everywhere defies the bar-line:

Ex.1

Schumann would not have taken the risk of shocking players by changing the time signature, but the real structure of his melody is obviously the following:

Ex.2

Situations of this kind are to be found everywhere in his music, as in the music of his closest successor, Brahms, and they are always a challenge to the performer.

The Symphonies

When in his early thirties Schumann turned to the serious problems of orchestral music and chamber music, he was still in the spring-time of his life. With a nature such as his, it was no mere chance that his first symphony had to be a Spring Symphony. In some piano works of his twenties – the three sonatas, the Fantasy in C major – he had tried his hand at larger concepts of shaping. But the perspective of the piano had kept such music within certain limits of form and sound. The prospect of the unlimited possibilities provided by the orchestra acted as a potent stimulus to his imagination; and behind this appeared the vision of a monumental structure such as a symphony after Beethoven and Schubert seemed to him to demand. A letter to his teacher of composition, Heinrich Dorn, is significant (14 April 1839):

Sometimes I would like to smash my piano, it has become too narrow for my thoughts. It is true that I still have so little experience of the orchestra, but I hope to arrive at this in due course. . . .

Not long afterwards an event took place which he reports to his fiancée Clara Wieck (11 December 1839):

Clara, today I was in the seventh heaven. There was a rehearsal of a symphony by Franz Schubert.[1] If only you had been present! It is indescribable, the instruments are men's and angels' voices, and everything is so full of life and spirit, and an orchestration defying Beethoven – and that length, that heavenly length! Like a novel in four volumes, longer than the Choral Symphony. I was utterly happy, and I would have wished for nothing but that you were my wife, and that I should be able to write such a symphony myself. . . .

He had tried his hand at orchestral composition long before. From 1832, the time of his earliest piano works that appeared in print (*Abegg Variations, Papillons, Paganini Studies*), dates a symphony in G minor, of which the first movement was actually performed at Zwickau, his birth place, at a concert in which Clara Wieck, then thirteen years old, took part as a soloist. Another performance, perhaps of the whole symphony, took place in Leipzig in June 1833. But Schumann discarded it from the list of his works, and we can be glad that editors have not made it a reason for creating confusion by renumbering his symphonies, as they have done in other similar cases. The score of the first two movements of this symphony was recently discovered, and it has actually been published. It is a typical beginner's work: genuine Schumannesque flashes of invention do occur, but the flow of events is broken by repetitive episodes and the scoring is in many places defective. The first movement suffers from an overindulgence in certain rhythmical patterns and a resulting lack of contrast, but Schumann's expressive melody comes into its own in the following Andantino, a songlike invention interrupted by an *Intermezzo quasi scherzo*. Only these two movements are available in score, and we do not even know for sure whether Schumann actually finished the whole symphony. But this early experience of hearing his orchestral music performed was certainly of the utmost value for him.

When his time to reach for the stars had arrived, Schumann's personal language was fully formed, and just as the subtlety of his piano style had been an immense asset for the songwriter, so the expressiveness of his vocal melody was a bridge to the 'voices of men and angels' he imagined he heard in the orchestra.

---

[1] It was the Great Symphony in C major, the manuscript of which Schumann had found in the house of Schubert's brother Ferdinand in Vienna, and sent to Mendelssohn, who performed this work for the first time at the Gewandhaus in Leipzig, eleven years after the composer's death.

SYMPHONY NO. 1 IN B FLAT MAJOR

As remarked above, Schumann had the habit of working on the inspiration of the moment, in one single, almost breathless effort. He sketched his First Symphony, Op. 38, in four days, between 23 and 26 January 1841, and the full score was finished on 20 February. 'The symphony has given me so many hours of sheer bliss', Schumann noted in his diary. 'I am full of thanks to my guardian angel who has let me finish a large work with such ease, within such a short time.' The first performance took place on 31 March in the Leipzig Gewandhaus, conducted by Mendelssohn.

Schumann's magic is his enthusiasm, his delight in a world of eternal spring; and this world is mirrored in his First Symphony. By instinct and intuition he fully realised the basic principle Beethoven had established in his symphonies and which Schubert had been the first to adopt in his own way: a symphony is a work of marked individuality, with a style of its own permeating all its parts. This gives its stamp to a cyclic work, unifying different and contrasting movements as if they were diverse manifestations of the same basic character. Symphonic individuality, most unmistakably to be found in great works such as Beethoven's *Eroica*, his Fifth Symphony, the Choral Symphony, or, not less strikingly, in his mature string quartets and sonatas, became an essential part of his legacy, a foremost quality of the symphony after Beethoven as represented by Schubert, Mendelssohn and Schumann, and it has remained the essence of symphonic style. With Berlioz and Liszt, by a most obvious misunderstanding of this feature of individuality, an extramusical suggestion, the 'programme', came into the symphonic structure. But as a general attribute of symphonic style a marked individuality of character has remained a prominent factor ever since. In Mendelssohn's mature symphonies – the *Scottish* and the *Italian* – it is suggested by a country landscape. In Schumann's symphonies, though the individual character is no less strikingly expressed, it is as difficult to define as it is in Beethoven's. In his First Symphony, however, he did find a term, calling it 'Spring Symphony'. One fact must be clearly understood: no word, no title can possibly comprise the infinite range of musical expression, and this is as true for 'Spring Symphony' as for, say, 'Heroic' or 'Pastoral', and this is a stumbling block on which programme music of all ages has foundered. Schumann must indeed have become conscious of the dubious value of such a title, as he omitted it when his symphony was published. It is certainly futile to look for programmatic features in music of such impeccable formal integrity. Just as Beethoven had done in his Pastoral Symphony, Schumann could have inscribed this work with the emblem 'More an expression of feeling than painting'. In fact, he used almost the same words when writing to Spohr about his symphony:

... Description and painting were not a part of my intention; but I believe that the time at which it came into existence may have influenced its shape and made it what it is.

He wrote more explicitly about this in a letter to Wilhelm Taubert in Berlin, who was preparing a performance of the symphony (10 January 1843):

Could you try to infiltrate some longing for spring into the playing of your orchestra? This is what I felt when I wrote it in February 1841. I would like the first entry of the trumpets to sound like a call from on high. Further on in the introduction I seem to be suggesting that everything is turning green, or that a butterfly is fluttering by, and in the *allegro* how gradually everything springlike is coming to life ... but these are fancies that came into my mind after having finished my work. ...

(If Schumann talked like this as a conductor, one can imagine how little patience his musicians must have had with him.)

Right from the beginning we are made aware of a momentous event to come:

Ex.3

There is a curious history behind this triumphant opening, showing how a beginner, who lacks practical experience with the orchestra, has to learn by trial and error. The first two bars, played by the trumpets and horns, originally stood a third lower:

Ex.4

At the first rehearsal the composer was shocked by the sound of the two notes G and A (marked by *x*) in the second bar; they came muffled and nasal, as against the splendour of the B♭, the opening and concluding note of the motif. The cause of this shock was that on the hand horn and natural trumpet – valve instruments were not yet in use in Leipzig – those two notes could only be produced in an artificial way, by 'stopping'. As this disadvantage no longer holds today, Schumann's original intention can easily be restored, as is often actually done nowadays. Schumann certainly remembered the rude shock. More than four years later he wrote to Mendelssohn, who was just preparing another performance of the symphony: 'Do you recollect the first rehearsal, in 1841, and the stopped trumpets and horns at the opening? It sounded like a violent cold in the head. . . .'

Schumann's approach to the problems of form is hardly less traditional than that of his predecessors, Schubert and Mendelssohn, as well as Spohr, whose symphonies, now long forgotten, were still prominent in the repertoire of the 1830s and 1840s. Schumann's own hallmark is a rapturous intensity of feeling, expressed in a concise melodic phrase, such as instrumental music had rarely known before him. He wears his heart on his sleeve and his enthusiasm is irresistible. Schubert conquers by the breadth of his melody, by its sweeping largeness and majesty, Schumann by the expressive intensity of a concise phrase and by the rapturous fervour he puts into it. A frequent expression mark to be found in his music is *innig*, a word difficult to translate and perhaps best rendered 'with intimate feeling'. A most characteristic example of this kind of melodic phrase into which Schumann puts all the fervour of his imagination is the song 'Mondnacht' (No. 5 of *Liederkreis*, to poems by Eichendorff). The piano puts in a short preface, two bars, repeated one octave lower. The following vocal phrase, reiterated five times during the short song, is its very essence, condensed into eight bars of ecstatic expressiveness (Ex. 5).

It cannot be denied that Schumann's precious capacity to pour all his soul into a phrase of four bars is not without a certain danger for the composer of symphonies. He has a deeply-rooted habit of using small building bricks, and he does this even when he is dealing with a large structure such as sonata form. Four- and eight-bar phrases are his chief units of invention, a habit acquired by the composer of more or less intimate piano music, and the

Ex.5

Es war als hätt_ der_ Him - mel die
Er - de still __ ge-küsst,

result is a genre painting when, as in the case of a symphonic movement, one would expect to find a large brush at work. Schumann's world is nearly everywhere confined, as it were, within the boundaries of a beautiful garden, fragrant and colourful. The great, majestic world of Beethoven or Schubert is not within his reach, just as it never was within the reach of Mendelssohn. Both have been reproached with this. The essential thing, however, is the sincerity and depth with which an artist reacts to the world within his view, and in this respect Schumann's music is a limpid mirror of an infinitely sensitive soul. In addition, one of its undeniable virtues is its extraordinary conciseness. What Schumann tells us is told in a succinct way. If Schubert's 'heavenly length' is not to be found in his music, there is never any diffuseness either.

His feeling for a shapely form, as for melody, is impeccable. The four movements of his Spring Symphony are beautiful individuals as well as ideal companions, together constituting a unified whole. The energetic first allegro, which follows a majestic introduction, and the lively, bustling finale are both in sonata form, with tightly constructed, closely knit expositions which demand and deserve the traditional repeat. The call of spring in the opening dotted motif has a basic function throughout the first movement, with an exquisite lyrical phrase thrown in as a second subject, and a concluding coda that flows into a rapturous new invention, a song of praise to divine nature.

Schumann follows his adored predecessor Schubert in the peculiar manner in which he likes to deal with the most dynamic part of the classical form, the development. As established by the great classics, Haydn, Mozart and Beethoven, it is the most incalculable, the most wayward part of the structure. Beethoven's acute sense of the essence of form is documented by the fact that only on one single occasion, in his Pastoral Symphony, did he cast a development in symmetrically restated episodes as in regular terraces, a natural result of the idyllic quietness of music that did not permit a development of the usual dramatic character, and so restricted all the necessary contrast to a colourful change of ancillary keys. This episodic type of development, often used by Schubert, appears almost regularly in Schumann's music. It suits his contemplative nature and his habit of inventing closely shaped phrases with a regular structure. Joined to lively modulation, this method provides him with all the contrast he needs. If it lacks dramatic impact, it always has the appeal of convincing spontaneity.

A less sophisticated type of construction – song form, da capo form – has its legitimate place in the two middle movements of a cyclic work, and this applies to the Larghetto and the Scherzo of the Spring Symphony. The former, a large, beautifully relaxed and expressive piece of music, has the fervour and melodic beauty of Schumann's finest songs. The heavy brass – trumpets and trombones – is omitted; the string orchestra displays its most lavish sound, with the divided first violins in octaves singing a love song. Tonal contrasts – C major, A major as against the E flat major of the movement – prevail in a more strongly accentuated middle section, until the song melody makes its reappearance on the oboe and ends with blissful quietness. The movement is concluded by a half-close, leading to the Scherzo. A serious, almost solemn invocation by the trombones prepares a transition. As in an improvisation, the opening fourth of the larghetto tune – B flat – E flat – resumed in the transition by the trombones, jumps to quite different conclusions as an extremely lively scherzo motif. As a subtle touch of tonality the tonic of the scherzo, G minor, makes just a fleeting appearance in the opening bar and instantly vanishes, reappearing again for the first time in a recapitulation. There are two trios, the first one in the dominant key, D major, changing the time to a capricious, very fast-moving two-four, the second in B flat, the relative major key. There is the traditional da capo of the scherzo section after the first trio; but after the second trio the joker seems to have become pensive. What follows is only a coda, dying softly away with a quotation from the first trio in the dominant key, D major. The tonic has asserted itself not as an ever-present fact but as the centre of events in a complicated system of gravitation, with the effect of a rich, colourful spectrum of harmony. In details of this kind Schumann reveals himself as a close contemporary of Wagner and a forerunner of Brahms, both most ingenious explorers of sophisticated tonal relationships.

The triumph of spring is reflected in a finale overflowing with life, adding to the pattern of events the lightness of a dance. Here, as in the first movement, an impeccably built sonata form ensures the necessary symphonic consistency. An episode of sheer poetry occurs before the start of the recapitulation, after a short but very dynamic development. There is a pause on the dominant, *poco adagio*. The horns dwell on the dominant seventh chord and the flute enters with a graceful cadenza, moving straight into the irresistibly happy rondo tune.

Schumann's First Symphony was an instant success, which is rare in any case, and quite especially so with a composer's first work for orchestra. It is incontestable that this is the most fortunate of Schumann's symphonies in the first impression it makes, and this applies as much to the youthful radiance of the music as to its brilliant sound, the most successful use of orchestral colour that Schumann ever succeeded in obtaining.

This paradox can be explained, as Tovey has pointed out in his programme notes to the Schumann symphonies. At the beginning of his activity as an orchestral composer, Schumann was under the influence of the Leipzig Gewandhaus Orchestra, playing under a first-rate conductor, Mendelssohn, who, at a time when orchestral musicians had only a casual and scanty training, contributed to it notably by founding the Leipzig Conservatoire, one of the first of its kind in Germany. Schumann, who assiduously attended Mendelssohn's rehearsals and performances, reacted to this stimulus in the proper way, relying on a disciplined string band and excellent wind soloists. He did the same in the first version of his Fourth Symphony, written shortly after the First, originally called *Symphonic Fantasy*, and first performed at Leipzig on 6 December 1841. It was not published, and he reworked and re-scored it ten years later at Düsseldorf. He performed it in this final version at the Rhenish Festival in May 1853. There can be no doubt that later orchestral impressions had an unfortunate effect on Schumann's manner of scoring, and most of all his own disappointments as a probably incompetent conductor at Düsseldorf, where he was in charge of a much less disciplined orchestra than Mendelssohn's at the Gewandhaus in Leipzig. A faithful pupil of Schumann's, Albert Dietrich, wrote about his master's orchestral style:

Schumann would always most strongly condemn any excess. If himself at the time of his activity in Düsseldorf used to overorchestrate by thick doublings, I am inclined to think that the fault was with the deficient violins of the Düsseldorf orchestra, whose thin sound he tried to cover by added wind instruments.

This observation is certainly correct.

Schumann's clumsy technique as a conductor and lack of alertness in reacting to faults or accidents became so obvious that he was in the end compelled to resign. That this took place not long before his definite mental collapse makes it likely that lack of concentration, a regular symptom of his ailment, was one of the principal causes of his failing. But the effect on his work of such experiences is obvious: he lost his self-confidence. One glance at the scores of Schumann's late years – his Third and Fourth Symphonies, his Violin Concerto and some of his overtures – reveals a desperate anxiousness to secure every melodic and harmonic detail by extensive doubling, the result of which is sometimes an oppressive dullness and sluggishness of sound. Schumann has always been abused for this and his scores have been subjected to arbitrary retouchings, most notably by Mahler who went rather far in this respect. The result was problematic because it implanted on Schumann's music a sound with which it did not agree. This happened at a time when, with Wagner, the symphonic poems of Strauss and the symphonies of Mahler, orchestral scoring had arrived at a brilliance never known before and when a generous splash of colour seemed essential to make an orchestral work worth listening to. Even in the earlier years of this century Max Reger, as conductor of the famous Meiningen orchestra, found it necessary to add retouchings to the scores of Brahms whose sound seemed to him not colourful enough.

Fortunately such abuse is a matter of the past. What a score of Schumann's demands is hardly ever an addition, but rather an occasional lightening of the texture by discreetly omitting redundant doublings in the woodwinds. The essential condition for obtaining a satisfactory sound in a Schumann symphony is impeccable exactness of every detail and perfect control of dynamics, something which, rarely obtainable formerly except under especially favourable circumstances, should nowadays be possible wherever a conductor takes the necessary care, as has been proven by so many excellent recordings. The chief reason, however, for problems of interpretation in Schumann's music is the prevailing homophony of his texture, which demands a kind of vocal flexibility of articulation in order to achieve the necessary spontaneity. Polyphonic elements add to the orchestral sound another dimension of incalculable value. One will realise this in comparing Schumann's symphonies with those of Brahms who, however, already represented a new generation in his use of orchestral colour. But as far as Schumann's manner of writing for orchestra is concerned, a faithful interpretation, stressing the melodic context with the necessary emphasis and without stiffness, will make a lot of difference. There is a peculiar effusiveness in his music, in his tendency of crossing barlines by syncopation and of blurring harmonies by anticipating or retarding inner parts. This involves a kind of constitutional *rubato* that contradicts a strict metronomic method. Freedom without exaggeration – this rule applies to everything pertaining to the interpretation of Schumann's music.

SYMPHONY NO. 2 IN C MAJOR

Schumann's Second Symphony, Op. 61, started in December 1845, but only finished nearly a year later, fell into a disturbed period of his life. His own words will best illustrate his situation at that time, although they obviously do not tell the whole story:

I sketched it at a time when I was ailing, and I may well state that it was, as it were, the power of resistance of the spirit that has influenced my work, and by which I have tried to prevail against my physical condition. The first movement is full of this fight, and in its character there is much of whimsical obstinacy.

Essentially, the spirit has prevailed indeed, right from the grand, solemn fanfare that opens the introduction:

Ex.6

Here is something truly symphonic, a gesture worthy to introduce a great work, and this fanfare will reappear not only towards the end of the first allegro, following the slow introduction, but, as a crowning gesture, again in the coda of the finale.

If the *allegro ma non troppo*, into which the introduction leads, docs not fulfil all our expectations, it is because its main subject – it has been foreshadowed in the introduction – runs dry with a repetitive insistence on a one-bar motif, which hardly permits a larger, more generous flow of events:

Ex.7

A melodically much more productive second subject, however, provides the necessary contrast, rounding off a well-shaped exposition, and it dominates the following development. The essence of the matter is, as pointed out above, the rareness of polyphonic elements in Schumann's orchestral texture. The dotted rhythm, in which the whole orchestra takes part, jogs on mercilessly. Schumann himself seems to have felt somewhat apologetic when he wrote to D. G. Otten, conductor of the Music Society in Hamburg, who was preparing a performance of the new work:

I wrote the symphony in December 1845 at a time when I was rather unwell, and I have a feeling that this may be evident. It was only in the last movement that I started to feel better, and when I had finished the work, I was well again. But as I have said: it reminds me of a dark period. It shows how sympathetic you are that such sounds of distress can appeal to you.

If the opening movement is not without certain dubious aspects, the following two movements, scherzo and adagio, are vintage Schumann. The dark cloud has passed. The scherzo, demanding virtuosity from the violins, has the zest of a perpetuum mobile, and two contrasting trios add a welcome touch of lyrical relief. With considerable changes in the last occurrence of the scherzo section, the movement is rounded off to make it one of Schumann's most thrilling orchestral inventions. Incidentally, it is not the usual three-four type of scherzo, but a kind of capriccio, such as Beethoven had already introduced into his late works. And Schumann has rightly understood that the best place for such a fast capriccio is between the first allegro and the adagio, contrasting with both and giving to a vigorous and lively finale the benefit of a strongly contrasting lyrical movement before.

This adagio in C minor contains some melancholy features. Its appeal – and this could be said of most of Schumann's slow movements – is its eloquent, fervent melody. And here the simplicity of the scoring contributes very much to the lyrical urgency of the music because the woodwind soloists – flute, oboe, clarinet and bassoon – have prominent parts in the distribution of colour. Once more, Schumann's scoring is impeccably transparent. The finale, on the other hand, is not without some problems. As in the first allegro the insistence on a frequently restated rhythmical pattern is an undeniable disadvantage. As a necessary contrast the fine, eloquent melody of the adagio is reintroduced as a second subject. Here again the woodwind soloists have important parts to play; and when towards the end the grand fanfare of the opening (6) again comes into its own, the circle is closed, and optimism has prevailed against uncontrollable, dark forces.

Such problematic periods were to recur again and again in the following years, that were mainly devoted to Schumann's largest, most ambitious works: the opera *Genovefa*, the cantata *Paradise and the Peri*, the music to Byron's *Manfred* and Scenes from Goethe's *Faust,* mentioned above.

SYMPHONY NO. 3 IN E FLAT MAJOR

It was only after his move to Düsseldorf in 1850 that Schumann became involved once more in the problems of a symphony. As a result of his rising fame as a composer he had, for the first time in his life, a prominent position as a conductor with large responsibilities. His predecessors in Düsseldorf, Mendelssohn and Ferdinand Hiller, had established a healthy and vigorous musical life. The Rhenish Festival, created in 1818 and connected with the Düsseldorf orchestra, offered a wide range of additional possibilities. In October 1850, shortly after his move to Düsseldorf, Schumann wrote his Cello Concerto, and on 9 December he finished the score of his Third Symphony, Op. 97, the most eloquent expression of a happy, creative disposition. It had its first performance in Düsseldorf on 6 February of the following year, conducted by the composer.

Schumann spoke of his new work as his 'Rhenish Symphony', but this title was omitted when the work was published, just as he had dropped the title 'Spring Symphony' with his first. However, the Rhenish scene, brimming over with life, is reflected in the whole work. And an interpolated fifth movement, actually a large, fully-rounded and concluded introduction to the finale, shows its meaning in the added inscription *In the character of a solemn ceremony*, which Schumann later withdrew. The ceremony alluded to was the promotion of the Archbishop of Cologne to the dignity of a cardinal, an event which had taken place during that year, and which the Schumanns had attended.

The Third Symphony is in Beethoven's heroic key, E flat major, and the opening theme is indeed heroic, a large invention, extending to twenty bars:

Ex.8

One must admit that the splendour of sound needed for this impressive start is not easily achieved in performance. The first

violin, the centre of events, starts with a subdued sound on the
A string, rising only in the third bar to the more sonorous E
string, and the flute and clarinet, doubling the melody, stiffen it
more than they invigorate it. The conductor has to keep a thick
quilt of harmony, that covers and dampens the soaring tune, under
strict control, and let the melody flow with a large phrasing, free
from narrow bar accents, to give it the sweeping swing it demands.

This movement is Schumann's most outstanding achievement
with regard to a true symphonic style. With that grand main theme
and a strikingly contrasting subsidiary idea of expressive beauty
the exposition grows into dimensions that do not permit the usual
repeat. The following development, drawing upon the whole
thematic material exposed before, moves through a thrilling circle
of events, leading to the entry of the recapitulation, on the tonic
six-four, with a burst of sound in which the opening theme, taken
up now by four horns in unison, arrives at its true splendour, and
the coda has still some surprises in store. Truly symphonic thematic
invention has proved its value.

The second movement, alive with a similar abundance of
inspiration, seems to point to the Rhenish scene with a happy
invention of folksong-like simplicity and straightforwardness.
It is entitled *Scherzo*, but has hardly anything in common with
the type of composition usually indicated by this term. Its rhythmical structure points rather to a sturdy, slowish minuet or *ländler*:

Ex.9

Here an aspect of Schumann's style has to be discussed which,
right from his early piano music, had always been an intrinsic part
of his artistic heritage: the German folk song. This had been of
central interest to artists ever since the seventeen-seventies, when
Goethe's friend Herder had published a critically annotated inter-
national collection of European folk poetry, *Stimmen der Völker
im Liede* (*Voice of the Peoples in Song*), emphasising the basic importance of folk poetry in the development of a poetic language. A
comprehensive collection of German folk poetry, *Des Knaben
Wunderhorn* (*The Lad's Magic Horn*), edited by A. Arnim and C.

Brentano (1806–8) became a lasting inspiration for German poets and musicians throughout the nineteenth century. It was followed in the 1830s and 1840s by publications of German folk tunes, of which one of the most enthusiastic collectors and editors, A. W. Zuccalmaglio, was a close friend of Schumann's. German folksong, still alive and unadulterated in the more remote German countryside at that time, is purely diatonic, sometimes modal, free from all chromaticism and untouched by melodic elements that could only develop against the background of harmony, such as modulations, suspensions or appoggiaturas. The folktune is alive in certain minuets and rondos by Haydn, who came from the Austrian countryside, and in the music of Beethoven and Schubert, who, as it were, came from Haydn. In Schumann's music it is an antidote to romantic exuberance and extravagant emotionality and it is a symptom of a healthy instinct that made him aware of certain dangers to which he felt exposed in less inspired moments. The folksong element is very noticeable in music of a youthful character such as *Scenes from Childhood* and *Album for the Young*, but one can detect its influence in many of his most happy inventions, for example in his songs to poems by Heine (*Dichterliebe*). The *Ländler* in his Third Symphony is a conspicuous illustration of this side of Schumann's style.

The form of the Ländler is peculiar. The tune is restated in a variation, followed by a contrasting idea. This leads to a modulating episode involving both motifs and is concluded by a recapitulation that softly evaporates. Nor does the following slow movement conform to the usual pattern: it is a graceful, songlike intermezzo, one of those tender pieces of Schumann's in which every phrase is filled with expression and the mood is *innig* throughout. After the heroic first movement and the sturdy *Scherzo* such an intermezzo was necessary as a contrast.

An interpolated movement, the 'Solemn Ceremony', widens the symphonic horizon in an unexpected direction. This is sacred music, grand and majestic (Ex. 10).

Built upon a single concise motif, it is similar to certain episodes in toccatas by Bach. The motif is diminished and augmented, goes through contrapuntal combinations, and moves in a large circle of modulation to a crowning climax with a gradual *diminuendo* towards the end. The aura of the Church is unmistakable. Schumann has here used an old motif, stemming from baroque style, and not

Ex.10

rare in Bach's music, for example in St Matthew's Passion (*Lass ihn kreuzigen*) and in the preludes in E flat major and B minor in the first book of the 'Forty-Eight'. Its background is the symbol of the cross, such as Pergolesi used unmistakably in the opening of his *Stabat mater*, with the two voices permanently crossing and re-crossing:

Ex.11

It is hardly necessary to add that at Schumann's time the symbolic meaning of this motif had long been forgotten. But traditions have a long life: the motif still survived in César Franck's symphony, with all its implicit solemnity.

Schumann's interlude is followed by one of his most energetic finales. And as if the Church were blessing the return to the joys of living, the solemn motif reappears again, transformed into a pliable contrapuntal phrase and asserting itself with marked insistence. This is without doubt a Rhenish symphony, and a work of glorious individuality.

SYMPHONY NO. 4 IN D MINOR

If his Third Symphony represents Schumann's closest approach to symphonic monumentality, the Fourth Symphony is his most ingenious experiment in form, an amazingly successful attempt at unifying the four movements of a cyclic work without altering their individual character and structure. Attempts at thematic unity were made by others before him. The most outstanding example, Schubert's 'Wanderer'-Fantasy, was certainly known to Schumann. His Fourth Symphony is more sophisticated as a construction and – this has been mentioned before – he was sufficiently conscious of its peculiarity of form to have originally called it 'Symphonic Fantasy', perhaps in remembrance of the 'Wanderer'-Fantasy. When he performed it again in Düsseldorf, in 1853, as his Fourth Symphony, he had written a new score. The substance had remained the same, although not without some minor adjustments. The orchestration, however, drastically changed, is hardly a success, thickening the texture by over-generous doublings, obviously with an anxious desire to make every entry as safe as possible. The negative result of such doublings, especially in octaves, which he inserted everywhere, is that they make a phrase, as it were, impersonal, lacking expressive individuality, and this is what a Schumann phrase cannot do without damage to its spontaneous expressive directness. The score of his Fourth Symphony in its final version is the most drastic illustration of Schumann's problematic experience as a conductor. It was Brahms who, with a full understanding of the problem, took the initiative in resurrecting the first version as an alternative, when the complete edition of Schumann's music was in progress, and Clara Schumann, his close friend, was very annoyed with Brahms, because she would not admit the possibility that Schumann could have rewritten a score without altogether improving it.

The dilemma is not too difficult to resolve. The original score – and this is what Brahms realised – is without any doubt preferable. Written shortly after the 'Spring'-Symphony, it shares its virtue of a limpid, transparent sound. But the final version contains two valuable improvements, the transition from the opening introduction to the first allegro, and the transition from the Scherzo to the Finale. These must certainly not be lost. The most practical solution would be to return to the first version – it has been published in the complete edition of Schumann's works – and to insert the two alterations mentioned. There is some more detail in the final version that could be regarded as an improvement. In any case a real 'final version' is needed, and is overdue, but this difficult task must be undertaken without prejudice and without pedantry.

The Schumann enthusiast has reasons to place this symphony at the top of the four. It is music of irresistible momentum, a marvellous union of continuous improvisation and close construction. And its four movements, linked by thematic threads, are in ideal balance and magnificently contrasted. It need hardly be added that the listener must not necessarily be conscious of these links: their virtue is plasticity of form in a sequence of events combining unity and diversity. Schubert's 'Wanderer'–Fantasy is shaped like an improvisation on a given theme, taken from his song 'The Wanderer'. In the slow movement this tune comes into its own as a theme with variations. In the other movements its opening motif appears in various disguises. In Schumann's symphony, the thematic lay-out progresses from one movement to another, new inventions emerging while the former ones reappear in variation as if it were an act of spontaneous recollection. Both works, with all their individual idiosyncrasies, are demonstrations of the inexhaustible vitality of the classical form-construction on which they are based.

Schumann starts, as Haydn liked to do and as he did himself in his first and second symphonies, with a slow introduction. A strongly-phrased motif in three-four extends to a large paragraph of twenty-eight bars, a symphonic prologue of majestic impressiveness. It will reveal itself later on as one of the main pillars of the building:

Ex.12

This introduction is not concluded, but runs *accelerando* into the following allegro, anticipating its main motif. Put into a closely-built phrase of four bars, this motif will turn out to be another foundation stone of the thematic structure. In the first movement it provides the concise main subject of a sonata form:

Ex.13

Succinct as the motif is, it is not conducive to a large, extensive form, and its continuous movement in semiquavers does not easily permit a stop. This causes the subsidiary section (as tradition demands it, in the relative major key) to draw on the same motif, as can frequently be found in Haydn's symphonies, and so the exposition, duly repeated, keeps within a narrowly confined thematic context. As will emerge in due course, this is not a deficiency but an asset, as it leaves to the following development the task of arriving at a huge, very impressive climax; and as the exposition has sufficiently presented its material, a recapitulation will prove unnecessary.

The development starts with a striking gesture by adding a sudden pause to the main motif which rises up in imitation. The trombones step in, opposing the busy main motif, and so we arrive at a climactic moment, the wind instruments calling up a new, rhythmically pregnant phrase against the semiquaver motif (Ex. 13) which now serves as an accompanying figure:

Ex.14

This is followed by the entry of a new, beautifully shaped melody, the first of this calibre to appear in the whole movement, an invention that could properly claim to be the real 'second subject', although it enters in the middle of the development:

Ex.15

The whole extensive progress of the development, from the entry of the trombones to the dynamic climax (Ex. 14) and the following expressive melody (Ex. 15) – it covers seventy-four bars, more than the whole exposition of the movement – reappears, exactly transposed a minor third higher. It has been pointed out that Schumann borrowed this method of development from Schubert. With the richness of invention offered here, the change of colour provided by the raised key is all that is needed for a convincing impression. A spacious coda concludes the movement, leading back to the tonic, D major, the semiquaver motif (Ex. 13) asserting its function as a cohesive element.

The second movement, in A minor, is a short but very suggestive episode. The oboe sings an elegiac melody; it could again be a folk-tune, a ballad. Until now every section of this work has contributed some new thematic stimulus. Now, with a return to three-four time and approximately the same speed as the first introduction, its motif (Ex. 12) sees an opportunity to return by adding an interlude to the ballad. And in a middle section, following it, the motif of the introduction expands into a soft, expressive tune, the solo violin paraphrasing it with a graceful figuration. The ballad returns and is concluded with a pause on A major, the dominant of the basic key of the symphony, D minor, which now returns in a robust scherzo. The main motif is new. Vigorously scored and supported by a bass in canonic imitation, it is another example of Schumann's folk-tune type of invention, and is strong enough to form the whole scherzo section. The trio, following it and changing the key to B flat major, turns out to be an old acquaintance: it uses as its main material the graceful figuration the solo violin had added to the motif of the introduction in the middle section of the 'Romanza', the slow movement, now putting on top of it a gently flowing song in the flutes and clarinets. Schumann here followed Beethoven's example – in his Fourth, Sixth and Seventh Symphonies – in letting the trio come once more after the da capo of the scherzo, which, however, is not to return a third time: the trio is slowed down, the figuration in the first violin gradually evaporates, and we arrive without interruption at a transition to the concluding finale, opening with a slow introduction. Once more, the semiquaver motif of the first movement makes a return, considerably slowed down. The trombones follow with an emphatic warning. But optimism prevails; with accelerated speed and ever-increasing liveliness of the rhythmical pattern we arrive at a colon: the finale, in the major tonic, opens in a mood of jubilant light-heartedness. And now we have come to yet another recapitulation: in the main subject of this finale in sonata form we recognise that climactic event in the development section of the first movement (Ex. 14). So the most impressive moment of the first allegro makes its return as the main subject of the finale! And with all that has happened in between, new perspectives are opened up and melodic invention offers as a second subject a new highlight:

Ex.16

More than in any other work by Schumann the finale is an ideal consummation of everything that has happened before. The richness of the exposition justifies its repetition, which Schumann added in the final version. A fugal episode provides a dynamic development, the recapitulation is cut short by moving directly to the subsidiary subject (Ex. 16), and an elaborate coda, introducing more and more shapely melody, arrives at a climax of enthusiasm.

Taking an overall view of Schumann's four symphonies, we have to put them historically between Beethoven and Brahms, as the first consistent and successful attempt to bring into the structure of the classical form a new variety of emotional impulsiveness and the picturesque background of a fresh, colourful world. Whether they happen to be favoured by fashion or not – at the present time they are certainly not – they have a legitimate place in the standard repertoire and they will maintain it. What keeps them alive is their impeccable, succinct form, youthful élan and abundant invention. It is a meaningful coincidence that their tonal initials, Bb, C, Eb, D, have reappeared, transposed one step higher, in the symphonies of his most legitimate successor, Brahms: C, D, F, E:

Ex.17

We may be permitted to take this as a symbol of a deeply rooted relationship.

OVERTURE, SCHERZO AND FINALE IN E MAJOR

An amiable symphonic parergon by Schumann deserves some attention. Op. 52, it is called 'Overture, Scherzo & Finale' and dates from the immensely productive year 1841, when his First and Fourth Symphonies (the first version of the latter) were written. The title is curious indeed, but it is exact and it shows the composer's unwillingness to use the term 'symphony', sanctified by Beethoven, for a less extensive and formally less comprehensive work. What is obviously missing is a slow movement. With all its charm and freshness this work has neither the grandeur nor the close-meshed form Schumann regarded as essential in a symphony. Whilst it is not of the same calibre as his four symphonies, 'Overture, Scherzo & Finale' is nevertheless one of his most attractive orchestral works.

At Schumann's time the term 'Overture' had already lost its primary meaning of an opening to a dramatic work, an opera or a play. For Beethoven this meaning was still valid and his overtures correspond to it: they were written for his opera *Leonore* (later *Fidelio*), for plays such as Collin's *Coriolanus*, for the ballet *Prometheus*, and for incidental music to Goethe's *Egmont* and Kotzebue's *King Stephen*. But already during Beethoven's lifetime his overtures were performed in orchestral programmes. And it was really not anything new when Mendelssohn created the Concert Overture as an independent type of composition with *A Midsummer Night's Dream* as his first contribution, many years before he actually wrote incidental music to Shakespeare's play. Nor was the title 'Overture' necessarily linked with a dramatic event for Schumann. For him it was a convenient term for indicating the form of a symphonic first movement, to which Mendelssohn's overtures had always adhered, just as much as had Beethoven's. In 'Overture, Scherzo & Finale' the opening movement starts with an informal introduction, based

upon a short lyrical phrase answered by an energetic one, the key
E major being defined by chromatically flavoured cadential steps.
Schumann found a peculiar, very personal way of letting a movement get into its stride: suggesting a motif tentatively, as it were,
to test its thematic and expressive potentiality by improvising till
it finds its proper scope. This is how this work begins, and one will
find similar openings in some of his other overtures, in his concert
pieces for piano and for violin and – this is perhaps the finest
introduction he ever wrote – in his oratorio *Paradise and the Peri*,
where, however, it does not spread out into an overture, but leads
to an opening recitativo. This style, this direct expression of feeling,
is like a self-portrait, Schumann himself as his friends have
described him: musing, meditating, absorbed in deep thought.

The allegro movement of 'Overture, Scherzo & Finale', following the slowish introduction, still starts on the dominant, *piano,*
gradually getting under way and forming a large, beautifully
expansive paragraph of thirty-six bars. A correspondingly large
bridge passage, in which the motif of the introduction plays a
certain part, leads to a second subject in the dominant key, B major.
But this is cut short, moving without noticeable punctuation to an
equally sketchy development that hardly deserves this designation,
being rather a kind of devious transition back to the recapitulation.
There are sonata movements by Mozart with no more than a hint
of a development, and in his Overture to *Le nozze di Figaro* the
development is replaced by a transition of sixteen bars. Schubert
did something very similar in his Overture to *Rosamunde*, which
Schumann certainly knew. It is quite likely that this was the reason
why he regarded this first movement more as an overture than as
the opening movement of a symphony, for which it seemed to him
to lack the necessary weight. This interpretation gains probability
if one also takes into consideration the fact that a slow movement,
according to Schumann's pensive, lyrical nature, was always his
most natural, congenial means of communication. The enigma of
its omission here seems to point to the above explanation.

If the first movement with all its truly Schumannesque charm
seems to belong more to a serenade than to a symphony, the
Scherzo and Finale are as symphonic as any corresponding movements in Schumann's symphonies. An obstinate dactylic rhythm
dominates the Scherzo (a pattern of rhythm Schumann had ex-
plored before in the concluding piece of *Kreisleriana*):

Ex.18

Such a device is not without some danger because the rhythm is liable to become stereotyped. Schumann was aware of this and opposed the narrowness of the dactyl by setting an expressive phrase on top of it:

Ex.19

Changing the key (C sharp) to D flat major, the enharmonically changed tonic, thirty-two bars (including repeats) of a gently flowing trio are all that is needed to give relief to the dactyl. And after a restatement of the scherzo that same trio, appearing again, melts into a poetic coda with a reminiscence of the Overture; the dactyl adds a humorously pointed conclusion.

Three trombones join the orchestra in the Finale, and they leave no doubt as to its symphonic character. A challenging entry of four bars introduces a vigorous theme which, when fugally treated, imparts to the whole movement a polyphonic energy rarely to be found in Schumann's music. It is an amply shaped sonata form and the development, taking up the fugal subject, moves in a large, colourful circle of modulation. Thematically as well as in its formal lay-out, this is the richest of the three movements, and this explains the composer's dilemma from which he escaped by the unassuming title 'Overture, Scherzo & Finale'. As to its sound, this work shares with Schumann's other orchestral works of the same year a style of orchestration which he unfortunately did not maintain, for reasons explained earlier.

What undoubtedly comes over here, as generally in Schumann's finales, is the impression of living in the best of all possible worlds. In this respect, he seems totally untainted by romantic gloom and pessimism. Considering this, the dark tragedy of his life appears still more ominous and disquieting. Was his ineradicable optimism an attempt to ignore the torturing symptoms of his impending doom? The riddles of the creative mind are insoluble.

The Overtures

A poetic meaning for an overture – originally an opening piece of a more or less neutral character – was a comparatively late phenomenon in its history. It was virtually invented by Gluck for his opera *Alceste*, and it remained a rather rare exception during the following decades. Even Rossini, half a century after Gluck, had no hesitation in using the overture of an *opera seria*, *Elisabetta*, for his *Barbiere di Siviglia*, a comic opera bubbling over with gaiety, which it fitted much better. Young Schubert, following Rossini's type of form, wrote two Italian Overtures without any suggestion of a subject, and Mendelssohn too could still write a piece (that has rightly been forgotten) with the random title 'Trumpet Overture'. It was different with Beethoven, who was very conscious of the poetic implications of an overture, although in a more or less general way. In this respect a tone-poetic event such as the trumpet signal in his Second and Third *Leonore* Overtures is an exception. Similarly in Mendelssohn's most outstanding contributions to this type of composition – *A Midsummer Night's Dream*, *Fingal's Cave*, *Calm Sea and Prosperous Voyage* and *Melusina* – the poetic background is suggested in a very general manner, within the limits of a clearly designed classical form. How simply this could be reconciled with a picturesque subject, inspired by two poems by Goethe, is shown in *Calm Sea and Prosperous Voyage*, where the calm sea is symbolised by a slow introduction and the prosperous voyage by the following allegro of a symphonic first movement. Nothing further was required.

Tone-poetic concepts in music have always been a subject of aesthetic discussion and dissension and they have a long history, going back as far as the sixteenth century. Among the early keyboard music by Bach we find a work with a naïve tone-poetic tendency, called 'Capriccio on the Departure of a Beloved Brother'. It consists of six short movements with quaint titles describing the whole succession of events, up to a concluding fugue on the postillion's horn signal. During the Napoleonic period a crude type of battle music became fashionable, and composers whose names have long been forgotten wrote 'Favourite Sonatas' on the battles of Neerwinden, Prague and Marengo, with marching armies, attacking fanfares and thundering guns, produced by both hands, arms and elbows of the player on the lower parts of the keyboard. Even Beethoven contributed to this species a work called 'Wellington's Victory, or the Battle of Vittoria', which at the time of the Vienna Congress (1814–15) was more successful than any of his symphonies.

Tendencies of this kind were revived during the romantic period and three prominent contemporaries of Schumann – Berlioz, Liszt and Wagner – were fully committed to the tone-poetic idea. Young Schumann, with his deep urge for poetic expressiveness, was certainly not averse to a picturesque background in music, as one can gather from his long, almost sensational article on Berlioz's *Symphonie fantastique* when this work was published (1835). There are moments in Schumann's early piano music where one cannot help thinking of an extra-musical idea, as for example with a kind of stage direction in the last movement of *Papillons*, Op. 2: *The noise of the Carnival night dies away. The church clock strikes six.* One may get this impression still more when one reads the following inscription over the final movement of *Davidsbündler* (in which Florestan and Eusebius, the fictitious representatives of Schumann himself, are featured): *In the end, Eusebius added the following, and an indescribable rapture radiated from his eyes.* Clara eliminated these inscriptions when she edited Schumann's piano works for the Complete Edition, and it is not unlikely that she acted according to

Schumann's own directions in this respect, as he may have found such oddities embarrassing when he read them again years later. But in all such cases – and the same holds of some fanciful titles in *Kinderscenen* or *Fantasiestücke* – one has the impression that the poetic suggestion, far from implying a 'programme', came as an afterthought, with the intention of giving the player a hint how to feel, how to interpret the music. This is indeed what Schumann himself suggested in a letter to Heinrich Dorn (5 September 1839), protesting against a Leipzig critic's derogatory remarks:

I have hardly seen anything as clumsy and stupid as what Rellstab [a critic in Leipzig] has written about 'Kinderscenen' ('Scenes from Childhood'). He seems to think I put a yelling child before me and try to turn this into music . . . But I do not deny that some children's faces were in my mind when I wrote that music. The titles, to be sure, came afterwards, and they are only discreet hints or suggestions for the performer's interpretation.

The same seems to apply to an inscription 'Voice from afar' in the last of his *Novellettes,* Op. 21, or to an intensely poetic moment in his *Humouresque,* Op. 29, where he puts an expressive inner part, called *Innere Stimme* ('Inner voice') into an intermediate stave in smaller notes, and leaves the decision to the player whether actually to play the melody, or to hint at it by discreetly accentuating single notes of the right or the left hand just as they occur (which I regard as the correct interpretation).

There is a sharp line dividing poetically inspired from actually programmatic music. The essential fact is whether the music has perfectly crystallised according to its own immanent laws, undisturbed by any 'programme'. Beethoven was very conscious of this when he put the motto quoted before at the head of his Pastoral Symphony. But there is still the Tempest in which programmatic elements certainly prevail. Nothing of this kind ever happened to Schumann who, in the face of increasing public discussion on this subject, took his stand with determination on the side of absolute music. At the time of Wagner's theoretical treatises (1849–52), which aroused much controversy, the discussion had become more and more acrimonious and dogmatic. Schumann was not actively involved, as he was no longer the editor of a music magazine; but his successor, Franz Brendel, now responsible for the Leipzig *Neue Zeitschrift für Musik*, was committed to the cause of Liszt and Wagner. A letter by Wagner, written to Theodor Uhlig, a friend of his in Dresden, reads like a party leader's instructions to his chief of propaganda:

You must always stick to the principle I have formulated in my letter to Brendel: to promote, advance and sponsor music whenever it moves towards poetic concepts, and criticise and condemn its erroneousness and defectiveness where it deviates from this line.

In Dresden the Schumanns had made the acquaintance of Wagner, conductor at the Court Opera, but without much mutual sympathy. With Wagner's theoretical pamphlets the gap between them had become unbridgeable. In his book *The Work of Art of the Future* (1850) Wagner had dealt radically with the whole subject of instrumental composition:

The concepts of form in which The Master [Beethoven] manifested his vision, his historic struggle for an ideal, remained for the composers of his time merely formal devices, becoming a kind of fashionable mannerism. And although no instrumental composer, making use of these forms, was able to arrive at any spark of invention, they never lost the courage of writing symphonies and suchlike music, without ever noticing that the ultimate symphony [Beethoven's Ninth] had already been written.

This disposed comprehensively of Schubert, Mendelssohn and Schumann. The character of the latter was sufficiently stubborn to ensure his adoption of exactly opposite principles, even if he had previously been undecided. His symphonies give a clear indication of this; they are an unconditional act of faith regarding classical form.

This principle applies equally to his overtures, although here a poetic element is certainly implicit in the whole conception. What he intended in an overture is clearly indicated in a letter to his young friend Joseph Joachim, who was at that time an ambitious composer, and had submitted to him a score of an Overture to *Hamlet*:

In reading your music I felt as though the scene were becoming visible, and Ophelia and Hamlet could be seen, true to life. You have conjured up everything that appeals both to the poetical and the musical sense in us.

He expected the educated listener to react in the proper way to a piece of music created by a poetic inspiration. With one single exception Schumann's overtures were written for dramatic subjects, and this also holds for his overture to Goethe's epic *Hermann and Dorothea*, which Schumann was at that time considering as a subject for an opera. Of his overtures, the one to *Manfred* has stood the test of durability without any doubt. The incidental music to Byron's drama, to which this overture belongs, consists largely of recitation to music, and this has always been an awkward proposition. Performances of the whole work have therefore remained rare events. The first stage performance of Byron's drama with Schumann's music took place at Weimar in 1852, conducted by Liszt. But the overture very soon made itself independent of the drama, and it is certainly the most impressive part of the music. It established itself as a concert overture, and has remained as such in the orchestral repertoire.

What about the listener's awareness of the actual poetic subject, Byron's drama? One must sadly admit that this condition, implicit in Schumann's above remarks, is all too rarely fulfilled. Is it really necessary? A romantic, a contemporary of Berlioz, Liszt and Wagner, was liable to overrate the poetic component in a musical impression. The *Manfred* Overture, an inspired, impeccable piece of music, can stand on its own.

The poetic background of the overture is a portrait of Byron's sombre, self-torturing hero, and this presented a problem to the composer, because it hardly permitted any contrasting mood, any brighter colour or reconciliatory gesture. Not without reason commentators have found a kind of self-identification by Schumann in the intensity with which he took to a subject of such agonising morbidity. There is hardly any necessity, however, to think of all this when we listen to a work of art of such purity and perfect balance of form and expression. Once more, the classical form has succeeded in objectifying a most problematic subject.

A slow introduction unravels step by step thematic threads which will later crystallise into concisely shaped subjects of a sonata form in a violently agitated movement. The introduction turns, as if searchingly, through wide spaces of chromatic modulation, till the hero emerges with a desperately passionate phrase:

Ex.20

The key, E flat minor, looks extravagant. But so is the hero, and it turns out that the resulting sound, owing to a permanent *vibrato* in the string instruments in a situation that hardly ever permits an open string, and also to an impeccably transparent use of the wind instruments, is of an extraordinary vitality and colourfulness. Together with his First Symphony and the first version of his Fourth, the *Manfred* Overture is Schumann's most successful orchestral achievement.

The febrile vehemence with which one phrase seems to pursue another, never permitting it to continue for more than a couple of bars, has resulted in a curious mannerism, unique in Schumann's music: for long stretches the melodic line proceeds by repeated short motifs – one bar, two bars – as if in a breathless attempt to make itself understood; here is one of these incidents:

Ex.21

This is certainly a dubious method of building. It has succeeded here owing to the magnificent impetus and strongly profiled form of the music. It is an odd coincidence that a late successor, coming with totally different premises and opposed to any dynamic function of form, arrived at the same mannerism of double phrases. One will find it everywhere in the music of Claude Debussy, most characteristically, for example, in *Nocturnes* and *La Mer*. Another mannerism of Schumann's, which is not easy to explain, is his fondness for syncopation, sometimes with an effect of gasping emotion, as at the very opening of the *Manfred* Overture. What it implies technically is an elimination of bar accents with a kind of emotional suspense resulting. It is one of the problems posed for the performer to deal with such syncopations in the most natural way, sometimes with a subtle touch of *rubato*. As has already been suggested, Schumann is no composer to be dealt with metronomically.

The fate of such a character as Manfred is death and annihilation. Schumann's music reaches its most suggestive depth of expression in the concluding coda, dying away with a gesture of hopeless resignation. Here is indeed a moment where romantic pessimism comes into its own, and romantic extravagance has found a congenial musical interpretation.

Nothing is as difficult to change as an established habit. Such a habit, maintained for a century and a half, was a strong, affirmative gesture to conclude an orchestral work, be it a symphony, a concerto, or an overture. The first to break this tradition was Beethoven in his Overture to *Coriolanus*, and it remained unique for a long time. Mendelssohn followed this example in his Overture to *A Midsummer Night's Dream*, and so did Schumann in his *Manfred* Overture. The impression on a receptive listener has always justified such a deviation from an established principle. It is worth remembering that Brahms was the first who dared to let the finale of a great symphony – his Third – die away in the softest *pianissimo,* and that Wagner's *Tristan and Isolde* and Verdi's *La forza del destino* were the first operas in which the same happened. And in all these cases the impression on the audience has proved deep and gripping, from the first performance to this day.

It is a sad fact that, as regards performance, all the other overtures by Schumann have become rare occurrences. The judgment of posterity expressed in this fact cannot be called unjust, because none of them is on the level of Schumann's highest achievements. The reason has been explained, and he himself hinted at it in that letter quoted in connection with his Second Symphony. Desperately needing the elation which only the creative act could give him, he would force his imagination to respond, and he accepted the result as his only available psychological self-defence. An overture was easier to throw off in one single concentrated effort than a symphony, and stimulating impressions were never lacking in an artist of such poetic susceptibility as Schumann. And with ever-increasing demands on new music by a successful composer, he was liable to let a less inspired work appear before the lapse of a necessary period of time could tell him the truth.

There are other causes underlying the failure of his only opera, *Genovefa*. For a composer who lived in Leipzig and Dresden, both towns with flourishing operatic activities, it would have been difficult to resist the alluring temptation of opera, just as it was for Schubert in Vienna two decades before. Both were unlucky in this respect, and probably owing to the same reasons: a basic lack of the dramatic sense and the necessary judgment of stage action as well as the problematical situation of German opera at that time. The libretto of *Genovefa*, whose subject Schumann took from a drama by Hebbel, he wrote himself in collaboration with the poet Robert Reinick. Wagner, conductor at the Court Opera in Dresden at that time, has told us in his autobiography of a meeting with Schumann, who read to him his libretto:

Sincerely anxious to assist him with the success of his work and to make him aware of its grave faults, suggesting to him the necessary modifications, I learnt something about the nature of this odd fellow. He would only permit me to be carried away by the subject of his enthusiasm, but stubbornly refused any interference.

If one thinks of the wretchedness of librettos of that period, even of successful operatic composers such as Spohr or Weber or Marschner, one will appreciate Wagner's sceptical point of view regarding the operas of his contemporaries.

The first performance of *Genovefa* in Leipzig (25 June 1850) seems to have been more or less a fiasco, and attempts at reviving the opera have remained rare and without success. Wagner was right, although his advice would hardly have saved the libretto, a clumsy dramatisation of an absurd subject, distantly related to the story of Weber's equally unfortunate *Euryanthe*. What interests us here is the overture, which, after *Manfred*, can claim the highest rank among Schumann's works of this type. He wrote it in a first burst of enthusiasm before he started work on the opera (1847), and it is an inspired, beautifully eloquent piece of music that did maintain itself in concert programmes, although with much less frequency than *Manfred*.

A slow introduction, giving the impression of a lonely monologue by the heroine, exposes tentatively a motif that will gain some importance in the following events:

It is of some interest to remember that this is a Wagnerian motif – *Lohengrin, Tristan, Parsifal* – and to realise that those two contemporaries, separated by an abyss, nevertheless had something in common in their artistic origins. The connecting link may have been Weber, who in the allegro of this overture seems to lurk behind the scenes. 'With passionate urgency' – this is the speed indication – a closely-grained movement is shaped, exposing some thematic material that will gain importance in the opera, most strikingly a fresh motif on hunting horns:

Ex.23

Here as in all his works of this type Schumann has maintained the integrity of the classical form, a jubilant peroration concluding the overture in accordance with the happy end of the story. As an additional virtue, the overture to *Genovefa* has the advantage of a colourful and limpid orchestral style.

Schumann was not deterred by the failure of his opera in Leipzig. This is shown by the fact that half a year later he was again in correspondence with an intended librettist, Richard Pohl, who later became one of the staunchest supporters of Wagner. The subject which he had in mind was Schiller's tragedy *The Bride of Messina*. The idea of an opera on this subject was abandoned, but it resulted in another concert overture which Schumann wrote in January 1851. Schiller's drama is a tragedy of fate, built on the ancient model of Sophocles and Euripides, with the chorus on the stage as a sententious witness of events. Something of this kind may be felt in Schumann's music, which could just as well have been given the title used later by Brahms, *Tragic Overture*. If not one of Schumann's outstanding works, it still deserves some attention as music of nobility and distinction. Written in the same form as the overtures to *Manfred* and *Genovefa*, a slow introduction leading to an allegro in sonata form, it is sterner in style, with a bare, severe sound, as seems to be implied by the subject. An exquisite melody in the clarinet, obviously intended to represent the main female character, Beatrice, may linger in the listener's memory:

Ex.24

Maintaining throughout a flow of characteristic invention, the work requires a closer acquaintance. It can be doubted whether one would think the same with respect to another nearly forgotten overture by Schumann, written to Shakespeare's *Julius Caesar*. It dates from 1851, the first year of his activity in Düsseldorf. Here the heroic style is treated with a large brush. The orchestra contains not only trombones but – the only time Schumann used this instrument – a bass tuba. The orchestral style is bold and more complex than usual with Schumann, frequently using curious blurring effects by combining straight and syncopated notes on top of each other:

Ex.25

Unfortunately the invention, tortuously moving through such impasses, has difficulties in arriving at anything substantial, and Schumann's usually reliable form-instinct has failed him in this case. Four times the opening subject, with a heroic gesture, starts on the tonic, F minor, over and over again, and no properly shaped second subject succeeds in breaking through. With no substantial exposition there is no proper development either, and when in the end we arrive at a triumphant peroration in the major key – is it Octavius, is it the spirit of great Caesar who has prevailed? – we cannot help feeling disappointed with the whole succession of events.

Schumann's years in Düsseldorf, a time of hectic activity and frequent spells of depression, are mirrored in an imposing list of works, with so many more or less questionable ones among them. Towards the end of 1851 he was again in contact with a prospective librettist, Moritz Horn, the poet of Schumann's cantata *The Rose's Pilgrimage*. Nothing came of the project. But Schumann's enthusiasm for the subject, Goethe's epic *Hermann and Dorothea*, went into an overture he wrote on the spur of the moment. So once more an overture destined for the theatre became a concert overture. Yet the music reveals unmistakably that it was not written as a symphonic work but as an introduction to the opening scene of an opera. It is strange that Schumann left it as it was, with a conclusion that lacks conclusiveness, ending quite obviously as if to a rising curtain. Still more puzzling, if one thinks of it, is an inevitable tone-poetic implication, given by the *Marseillaise,* which, from the beginning right to the end, seems to dominate the events. It is true, the French Revolution, which this tune unmistakably suggests, plays its part as a background of Goethe's poem. But this is a peaceful idyll in the Rhenish countryside where the arrival of a convoy of refugees from the French side of the Rhine, in 1793, creates some excitement, and accidentally brings the two lovers, Hermann and Dorothea, together.

Schumann was fond of the *Marseillaise*. He had used it, twelve years before, in one of his works for piano, *A Carnival Prank from Vienna*, camouflaging it in six-eight for the fun of fooling the censor, as that tune was strictly forbidden in Vienna. To give it such prominence in the thematic lay-out of an overture to *Hermann and Dorothea* puts an incomprehensible emphasis on a dramatic background motif, whereas it would be perfectly in place in an introduction to an opening scene in which, with the arrival of the refugees, this motif could play a prominent part. Cases of a similar kind are not rare in opera. We may think, for example, of the orchestral preludes of all the four parts of Wagner's Tetralogy: the waves of the Rhine in *Rheingold*, a tempest in *Die Walküre,* musing and tinkering Mime in *Siegfried*, and the nightly solitude of the Norns in *Götterdämmerung*. The meaning of such a prelude is concentrated on the opening scene, and the same seems to be the case with the overture to *Hermann and Dorothea*. It was published after Schumann's death. He may not have intended to present it as a concert overture. It is a subtle, thoughtful piece of music, and *Hermann and Dorothea* might have become an attractive *Singspiel*; this seems to have been what Schumann intended. With a tolerable libretto, it might have succeeded better than the unfortunate *Genovefa*.

Much less appealing is a concert overture for choir and orchestra, written for some special occasion in Düsseldorf and called *Festival Overture on the Rhine Wine Song*. It dates from April 1853. In the Rhineland the precious wine produced there is an object of quasi-religious feelings and celebrated in innumerable songs. The one used by Schumann enjoyed a tremendous popularity in the Rhineland and belongs typically to the *Liedertafel* (gleeclub) style, cultivated by German male choruses of a popular type, and still alive, I am afraid. One may think of the *Academic Festival Overture* by Brahms, based on tunes that are hardly more distinguished. He succeeded in making them palatable by paraphrasing them with incomparable subtlety. It is true that the bluntness of such a tune becomes still more obtrusive when it is joined by equally blunt words. Such cases offer clear illustrations of the tremendous difference between a folk-song and such popular songs. The opening part of Schumann's overture is a festive introduction, suitable for an event of pomp and circumstance. He may have thought of Beethoven's Choral Fantasia, he may even have thought of Beethoven's Choral Symphony, when he prefaced the choir by a tenor solo, inviting all the brothers to sing the praise of Rhine wine. Florestan, of blessed memory, would have looked askance at such fraternisation with the Philistines.

From the same year, 1853, dates Schumann's last overture. He wrote it as the last instalment of a work that had kept him busy for a number of years, 'Scenes from Goethe's *Faust*', a succession of various dramatic, lyrical, meditative and transcendental episodes taken from Goethe's great dramatic poem, resulting in a kind of monumental oratorio. As has been stated before, the overture was one of the problematic products of that critical year, and it has rarely been used as a concert overture. It is, however, hardly dispensable in a performance of the *Faust* Scenes, a great work that demands an impressive prelude. It starts impressively indeed with a sombre introduction, portraying Faust as a brooding introvert and profound thinker. In the following allegro with its violent, moody passion we may think of Faust's lifelong quest for truth, for an ideal. It is a restless piece of music, with hardly a moment of relaxation. The trouble is that it remains a gesture, a desperate struggle for an inspiration that refuses to materialise. It is a tortured piece, the phrasing rarely exceeding one bar, the expression of a heroic will to prevail and a tragic refusal of the creative spirit to give its blessing. And the less space the thematic substance succeeds in covering, the more instruments are packed into it, resulting in a grey monotony of sound. Nor does one feel a relief when towards the end the major tonic breaks through, with an attitude of heroic triumph; it remains a gesture, the invention failing to take wing. All the same, there is something venerable in this struggle to the last, in this effort of a great mind to fulfil its destiny. The man who wrote this was indeed a Faust in spirit.

The Concertos

PIANO CONCERTO IN A MINOR

Schumann's restlessness was Faustian too. He was blessed, however, with a family life of undisturbed peace and happiness. When he first met Clara, the daughter of his piano teacher Friedrich Wieck, she was a child of eleven, an infant prodigy and her father's pride and most brilliant pupil. Seven years later a tender relationship had developed between the young people, but father Wieck refused his consent, and only in 1840, after a decision by a court of law against the father's objection, could the marriage take place. Meanwhile Clara had become one of the most successful pianists of her time. Her personality and manner of playing certainly had a decisive influence on Schumann's piano style; and his whole attitude as a musician and individuality as a composer had surely contributed in shaping Clara's character as an artist. His great predecessors Mozart, Beethoven, Weber and Schubert had written their piano music for their own hands and were the first to play it. Schumann, with his crippled hand, projected all his enthusiasm as a potential virtuoso to his ideal interpreter, Clara. This unique and beautiful relationship between a composer and a performer is expressed in everything Schumann wrote for his favourite instrument, in great solo works such as *Kreisleriana, Carnival,* or *Symphonic Studies* just as in his Piano Quintet and Piano Quartet. And its most glorious consummation is Schumann's Piano Concerto, Op. 54, the composer's loving homage to his wife, the virtuoso.

The concerto is one of the most felicitous and stimulating form-constructions within the classical tradition. It combines the consistency of a symphonic work with a specific purpose: to give a brilliant virtuoso an opportunity to make an impressive appearance as the centre of events and to offer the necessary scope for technical display. Technical brilliance had always been an essential component of a concerto. This already applies to Bach's works of this type, as well as to Mozart's or Beethoven's. But in all these cases the virtuoso component is in an ideal balance with the symphonic aspects of form and texture. The situation became different when at Beethoven's time, and still more so after him, instrumental virtuosity developed as never before. With great violinists such as Paganini, Rode, Kreutzer and Molique, and great pianists such as Hummel, Liszt, Kalkbrenner, Thalberg and Herz, the virtuoso concerto was established, written by brilliant players for their own hands, with a dazzling display of individual features of technique. Chopin, who started his career as a pianist, adopted the virtuoso style of piano writing and turned it into a unique language of his own. Schumann, the critic, supported Chopin with enthusiasm right from the first work of his that came into his hands. But he was violently opposed to the shallow exhibitionism of pianist-composers such as Herz and they became the favourite subjects of his critical attacks.

It was, however, not Schumann the critic who succeeded in proclaiming to the world the essential qualities of a concerto but Schumann the creative artist, whose Piano Concerto has remained a standard work of its kind, one of the greatest that came after Beethoven. Its first movement was written during a tremendously productive year, 1841, the year of Schumann's first symphonic achievements. He called it 'Concerto Fantasy', but he may already have had second thoughts about it at that time, as he did not have it performed. He did, however, try in vain to find a publisher for the Concerto Fantasy, and this disappointment may have caused him, for the time being, to lay it aside. Four years later, in July 1845, he completed the concerto by adding an Intermezzo (*Andantino grazioso*) and a Finale (*Allegro vivace*). Its first performance took place in January 1845 in Dresden, played by Clara and conducted by Ferdinand Hiller. Shortly afterwards Clara played it at the Gewandhaus in Leipzig, with Mendelssohn conducting, and, following this, also in Prague and Vienna. It was an instant success, was taken up in turn by other outstanding pianists, and even during his lifetime became one of Schumann's most frequently performed works.

His piano style, though demanding the bravura of a virtuoso, never makes any sacrifice to superficial brilliance, and this also holds of his Piano Concerto. Its splendour of sound results from a wonderful combination of expressive urgency and relaxed melodic eloquence, and this is indeed the essence of Schumann's style. Paradoxically, the first movement, originally called 'Fantasy', follows with the utmost fidelity the basic pattern of a traditional first movement of a concerto, taking advantage of the example given by Beethoven in his last two piano concertos, in G major and E flat major, of introducing the soloist with a kind of preface right at the beginning, before the traditional tutti. Schumann's only divergence from the classical form-pattern was that he cut the opening tutti altogether, a concise exposition traditional in a concerto. Just as in the first movement of a sonata or a symphony the exposition is repeated, in a classical concerto the tutti, given to the orchestra, provides a succinct exposition of the thematic material, which then, with the concurrence of the solo instrument, is restated in a larger, more brilliant and expansive way. In Schumann's Concerto the piano and the orchestra are combined right from the beginning. The main subject, following a turbulent opening of a few bars, is a tenderly expressive lyrical statement (Ex. 26 overleaf).

One would hardly expect any dynamic possibilities from such a quiet song-melody. But it instantly takes wing and remains the centre of events throughout the whole movement with an ever-

Ex.26

increasing expressive urgency. There is a continuous dramatic dialogue between the solo and the orchestra, and, as so often with Haydn, the opening motif (*x* in Ex. 26) also provides the substance of a subsidiary subject, an enthusiastically eloquent phrase. The most magical moment occurs at the beginning of the development, when the first three bars of the subject, started by the piano and continued by the clarinet, introduce an episode of rapturous delight:

Ex.27

Andante espressivo

There is something improvisatory in the slowing down and rhythmical transformation of the subject, and this is in line with the general character of a movement which, although built as a sonata form, has all the freedom and spontaneity of a fantasy. One can see why Schumann was at first inclined to call it so. The lyrical episode is broken off by a violent clash between the solo and the orchestra, opposing each other with the turbulent motif with which the movement had started, and this gives a necessary respite to the protean main subject before it returns in a new disguise, growing now into a large paragraph of twenty-four bars which, transposed a fourth higher – once more the Schubertian trick of building a development! – move with a long *diminuendo* and *ritardando* to the recapitulation.

The cadenza of the solo instrument, put in the traditional place before the concluding coda, is a closely-built structure of ideal thematic consistency. Here too, Schumann has followed the example given by Beethoven in his Piano Concerto in E flat of treating the cadenza not as an *ad libitum* improvisation but as an integral part of the composition. Without any incident of superficial virtuosity Schumann's cadenza, magnificently constructed, forms the real top of the building.

After the great events of the first movement, the Intermezzo (*Andantino grazioso*) and Finale (*Allegro vivace*) are relaxed and amiable, closely and concisely built and gloriously contrasted. The Intermezzo is a quietly meditative song, or rather a duet for alternating voices, with a tender tenor solo in the cellos dominating the events. The Finale, into which it leads without interruption, is a radiantly communicative and optimistic expression of unclouded happiness. Here Schumann has made use of another Schubertian trick, characteristic of a composer who is accustomed to finding everything essential in the invention itself: by starting the recapitulation of the exposition, first concluded on the dominant, in the subdominant key, he arrives in the end at the tonic without having to change anything except for exactly transposing, and concludes and crowns it by a coda of irresistible momentum.

A recurring episode of the Finale – the second subject – involves a certain difficulty for the performers: Schumann's mannerism of syncopating here leads to a dangerous ambiguity, because a regular sequence in a two-four pattern, set against the three-four beat, is liable to create an annoying rhythmical monotony if it is not counteracted by a discreet stressing of the obliterated bar structure (Ex. 28 overleaf). This episode is a well-known danger-corner for the accompanying orchestra, which otherwise does not present any problems of technique or sound.

Ex.28

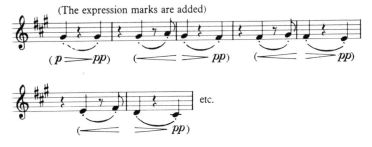

(The expression marks are added)

OTHER WORKS FOR PIANO AND ORCHESTRA

Whatever Schumann wrote for piano was written with love for the instrument and for his ideal interpreter. This is certainly true of two smaller compositions for piano and orchestra, written for Clara: *Introduction and Allegro appassionato,* Op. 92, and *Concert Allegro with Introduction,* Op. 134, dedicated to Brahms. Both are works of distinction, and the first of them particularly deserves more attention from performers than it actually receives. The trouble is that pieces of this kind, lasting hardly a quarter of an hour, fit badly into our standardised concert programmes. *Introduction and Allegro appassionato* was written in 1849, another very productive year for Schumann, largely devoted to vocal and dramatic music (*Requiem for Mignon,* Scenes from Goethe's *Faust, Manfred,* and many songs). There is indeed a hint of vocal urgency and expressiveness in the main thematic suggestion of the Introduction, an exquisitely beautiful horn call, which is to retain an important function in the following allegro, a freely treated sonata form with thematic material of charm and character. The piano is always in the foreground, now leading, now with subtle accompaniments, and the orchestral writing is sonorous and colourful. Though a work of much smaller dimensions than a concerto, it is a rewarding task for a virtuoso. The *Concert Allegro with Introduction,* less distinguished in its thematic content, is not quite unaffected by the unrest of that last year of Schumann's creative activity, 1853, when it was written as a gift to Clara in celebration of their fourteenth wedding anniversary. The introduction is hardly more than a short prelude in the character of an improvisa-

tion. It leads to an allegro in the form of a concerto first movement. The pianistic style is subtle and rich, and the piece culminates
in an elaborate cadenza with a brilliant and effective conclusion.
This work too would deserve to be better known than it actually is.

KONZERTSTÜCK IN F

FANTASY IN C

The same thing applies still more to two works by Schumann
that have almost disappeared from concert programmes:
Konzertstück for four horns and orchestra, Op. 86, and *Fantasy* for
violin and orchestra, Op. 131. The former was written in February
1849 in Dresden, where Schumann lived at that time as a choral
conductor, and it was probably stimulated by the excellent quality
of the Dresden orchestra. Schumann's activity there, however,
was interrupted by the revolutionary events of that year – Wagner
was actively involved in them – and the first performance of the
new work took place at the Leipzig Gewandhaus one year later.
Schumann was fond of it. 'It seems to me to be one of my best
pieces', he wrote to Ferdinand Hiller (10 April 1849). It is certainly
one of his most neglected; performances are rare events. This
Konzertstück is a fully fledged concerto, three independent movements linked by transitions, and it has a magnificent sound, taking
advantage of a very unusual range of thematic and contrapuntal
possibilities. It is indeed a unique specimen of its kind and should
be welcome wherever a horn quartet of appropriate quality is to be
found. The four horns are accompanied by a large orchestra,
including a piccolo and three trombones. Starting with a fanfare
by the four horns, one of its main thematic suggestions, the opening
movement develops as a sonata form with a colourful variety of
combinations offered by the peculiar proposition, the four soloists
competing with each other melodically and contrapuntally, and
the orchestra adding trenchant points and interludes of its own.
As so often with Schumann, the solo group enters right at the
beginning, discarding the traditional tutti. The orchestra, taking
up the fanfare and enlarging it into a full thematic statement, is
followed by a new entry by the four horns who take the lead in
a magnificent competition of thematic suggestions in one of the
most adventurous and elaborate first movements written by
Schumann. Fully developed and concluded by a pause, it is

followed by a slow intermezzo, called *Romanza* (*Ziemlich langsam, aber ohne zu schleppen* – Rather slow but without dragging). It is songlike, as are so many of Schumann's slow movements. But here again, owing to the unusual circumstances, unusual combinations emerge. The second and larger part of a shapely melody is formed as a canon, sung by the first and second horns. An expressive climax is reached in a quiet middle section in ternary form, the orchestra and the horn quartet taking turns. A shortened recapitulation leads to the finale – *molto vivace*, another energetically shaped sonata form. As if the contending forces, the solo group and the orchestra, had learnt from their previous experience, the fanciful interplay arrives at its climax in an adventurous development with far-flung tonal diversions. It is one of Schumann's most thrilling finales, and it determines the extraordinary quality of a work that has been unaccountably forgotten. Perhaps even unconsciously, he has succeeded here in reviving the most stimulating form device of the baroque period, the *concerto grosso* with its ample thematic lay-out, based upon the confrontation of tutti and solo motifs, and a large form resulting from such rich material.

Schumann's *Fantasy* for violin and orchestra, Op. 131, written in 1853, does not deserve its total neglect either. If not of the same calibre as the *Konzertstück* for four horns, it is nevertheless a distinguished composition, written for and dedicated to one of Schumann's most faithful young friends and disciples, Joseph Joachim, who always kept it in his repertoire. It has an appeal of intimate expressiveness and a capricious charm of its own. As the accompaniment is largely given to the string group, leaving to the full orchestra the task of incisive tuttis, the solo violin can easily remain in the foreground. In this respect the great violinist may have been the composer's expert adviser. A slowish prelude in A minor introduces an energetic allegro in C major, built like a concerto first movement, with strong thematic contrasts, concisely shaped and rounded off by an elaborate cadenza. It certainly does not lack technical brilliance and effectiveness. But since this work too lasts less than a quarter of an hour, it shares with the concert pieces for piano the disadvantage of fitting badly into our usual concert programmes.

CELLO CONCERTO IN A MINOR

It is less easy to account for the comparative neglect of Schumann's Cello Concerto, Op. 129, a masterpiece indeed. Considering the scarcity of cello concertos that have a right to claim the same distinction, Schumann's should have a place in every cellist's standard repertoire. Written in October 1850, just after his move to Düsseldorf, it shortly preceded his Rhenish Symphony. Both works, with their strong individuality and abundance of inspiration, are symptomatic of one of the happiest, most contented periods in Schumann's life, with a new and immensely stimulating sphere of activity. Unfortunately this happy mood was not of long duration.

The Cello Concerto shares its key, A minor, with Schumann's Piano Concerto, but it has a totally different character, according to the nature of the instrument. As in the *Konzertstück* for four horns, the three movements are linked by transitions. In fact, Schumann first called it *Konzertstück*, obviously in doubt whether he should use the more pretentious term 'Concerto', and this may have been due to the modest size of the work; its duration is less than twenty-five minutes, although it has both the sweeping greatness of style and the technical brilliance one expects from a concerto. Schumann shows a much better instinctive understanding of the cello and the secrets of its nature than of the violin, with which he occasionally committed errors of judgment regarding its sound in different positions and its technical peculiarities. He never played a string instrument properly. But after the mishap with his right hand, in 1832, when he had to give up his pianistic efforts, he dabbled for a time with the cello, as he found that he was able to handle the bow in spite of a paralysed finger on his right hand. He gave it up very soon, but it seems that even this fleeting acquaintance with the instrument was of lasting value. His chamber music, for example his Piano Quintet, offers ample illustrations of his treatment of both the violin and the violoncello.

The first movement of the Cello Concerto, again discarding the traditional tutti, introduces the solo instrument after four bars of a simple orchestral cadence, with a large, sweepingly phrased melody (Ex. 29 overleaf). It expands into a paragraph of thirty bars, presenting the solo instrument in its most attractive function, as a tenor. The orchestra follows with vigorous accents, leading to the relative major key, C, and to another entry of the solo with a chromatically

Ex.29

Allegro ma non troppo

suffused countersubject. The necessary technical display, in passages of triplets, is added in a lively codetta. So far the solo instrument has remained dominant. In the course of the following, dynamically moving development it assumes the function of a melodic bass to the softly tuned orchestral parts, arriving, as a lyrical intermission, at the main subject (Ex. 29) in a far distant key, F sharp minor, then turning the triplet passages of the codetta into a bridge back to the tonic and to a recapitulation that adds some melodic variations to the restated exposition.

It seems that Schumann, the tone-poet with a strong feeling for the emotional unity of his work, had a natural aversion to the interruption caused by the conclusions of individual movements of a concerto, followed as they were by the customary applause, a practice which was not generally eliminated until a century later. The first movement of his Piano Concerto, originally written as an independent composition, kept its conclusion. But in the following *Intermezzo* as in all his concert pieces, including the one for four horns with its three independent movements, he consistently avoided conclusions, as also in his Cello Concerto. A result of this is the shifting of the customary cadenza, a solo episode in free, improvisatory style, to the finale. A gradually retarding coda of the first movement leads without interruption to the slow movement (*lento*) which, though only extending to thirty bars – this is the cause of the short duration of this work – achieves a glorious climax of inspired singing, the solo cello again assuming the function of a tenor, and leading with an accelerating coloratura passage to a fast-moving, capricious finale (*molto vivace*) in which the solo cello, true to its character, again finds opportunities for singing interludes. Like the first movement the finale is in sonata form, moving towards the end to the major tonic, A, and into the above-mentioned cadenza. Though in accordance with the rhapsodic style of an incident of this kind, it gives the orchestra a chance to participate with intermittent accompaniments, contributing significantly to the impressive appearance of the solo cello which otherwise, especially on its lowest string, is so easily in danger of sounding rough. Indeed, everything in this extraordinary work contributes to a grand impression. The only thing to be regretted is that occasions for enjoying it are not frequent enough.

A PARERGON

In 1937, more than eighty years after Schumann's death, a work was added to the list of his concertos, and this publication has a bizarre history. In autumn 1853, a few months before his mental breakdown, he wrote a violin concerto, his last finished composition. When after his death a number of manuscript works of his were published, his widow, Clara, and her most competent and trusted friends, Joachim and Brahms, decided to leave the Violin Concerto unpublished. They acted according to their conscience and after the most serious consideration of all relevant circumstances. The same decision was made when in the 1880s – the last volume appeared in 1893 – a Complete Edition of Schumann's works, supervised by Clara, was prepared. One could not put the facts more succinctly and more reverently than Joachim did, a number of years after the event. He, whom Schumann intended to be the first performer of his concerto and who was the first to see the score (which remained in his hands), wrote to his friend and biographer, Andreas Moser (5 August 1898):[1]

... You ask me for information about a manuscript of a violin concerto by Robert Schumann which is in my possession. I cannot speak about it without emotion, for it dates from the last six months before the mental illness of my dear master and friend. ... The fact that it has never been published will be enough to lead you to the conclusion that it is not worthy to rank with his many magnificent creations. A new Violin Concerto by Schumann – with what delight would all our colleagues greet it! And yet no conscientious friend, concerned with the fame of our beloved composer, would ever mention the word 'publication', however eagerly the publishers might call for it. For it must be regretfully admitted that there are unmistakable signs of a certain weariness, though his intellectual energy still strives to master it. Some passages indeed

[1] Translation from *The Musician's World*, ed. Hans Gal (Thames & Hudson, London, 1965).

(how could it be otherwise?) give evidence of the profound spirit of its creator; but this makes the contrast with the work as a whole all the more depressing.

The first movement has something wayward about its rhythm, sometimes starting off impetuously, sometimes stopping short in obstinacy; in the first *tutti* this is effective, as a rapid introduction to a second, gentle theme with a beautiful soft melody – genuine Schumann! But this is not developed into anything really refreshing . . . The second movement begins with a characteristic passage of deep feeling, leading up to an expressive melody for the violin. Glorious Master – the blissful dream is captured, as warm and intimate as ever! But though my heart bleeds to say so, this blossoming fantasy gives way to sickly brooding, the stream stagnates, though the theme meanders on; and then, as though the composer himself were yearning to escape from this drab introspection, he rallies himself, hastening the tempo, for a transition to the final movement. . . . The main theme is introduced with great energy, but as it develops it becomes monotonous, again taking on a certain ominous rigidity of rhythm. Even in this movement, however, there are interesting points of detail. . . . But here again there is no sense of spontaneous enjoyment. . . . One can see that the thing is being carried forward by habit rather than soaring in happiness. . . .

Now that I have satisfied your wish to be told something about the concerto, my dear Moser, you will understand why you had to press me so often. One is always reluctant to turn the light of reason in a direction where one has been accustomed to love and adore with all one's heart. . . .

As Joachim's letters were published in a large collection containing the above one, it is more than likely that this letter led to the 'discovery' of Schumann's Violin Concerto by Jelly d'Arányi, a grand-niece of Joachim, and herself a reputed violinist. Allegedly she was made aware of its existence by the spirits of Schumann and Joachim in the course of a spiritualistic séance, of table-moving. Everything else was done by a publisher who expected substantial success from an unaccountably forgotten masterpiece. The 'discoverer's' ambition of securing a sensational first performance, a world première, was frustrated owing to peculiar circumstances, but the concerto duly appeared, had a number of performances and has been on the shelf ever since, except for rare reappearances.

There is not much to be added to the above explanations by a great musician, one of the foremost violinists of his time, a close friend and an unrivalled expert of Schumann's music. Joachim's description, discreet as it is, gives a fair account of the relevant facts. The problematical quality of Schumann's creative work at periods of a morbid indisposition was explained above. His self-defence against attacks of the tormenting discomfort connected with his disease was frantic work, creative effort giving him the illusion of an escape. His lavish inspiration had so often enabled him to throw off a great work in a miraculously short time. The acquired habit of such speed became a danger at certain critical periods that were to occur more and more frequently during his later years when his stubborn energy was liable to become stronger than his critical control. The Violin Concerto is a tragic document of a desperate struggle against inexorable fate.

According to his diary Schumann started the composition of his work on 21 September 1853, and finished the full score twelve days later, on 3 October. The three movements – *Vigoroso ma non troppo allegro, Lento,* leading to *Vivace ma non troppo* – suffer from the same deficiency: fragmentary and therefore repetitive thematic material. A sturdy motif, which begins the first movement, tries over and over again to assert itself and does not succeed. The same applies still more obviously to an expressive second subject – Joachim mentions it affectionately – because it limits itself to a one-bar-phrase, restated over and over again in sequence. And the solo violin, trying to arrive at an effective technical display, remains restricted to an empty formalism. The second movement, keeping both thematically and tonally within the narrowest confines, nevertheless has a genuine appeal with its shapely melodic strands. The solo violin enters with an intimately expressive motif that seems to promise a wider melodic horizon, but it seems unable to unfold properly and becomes bogged down in short phrases. The finale, into which it moves without interruption, is a kind of *polacca*, where once more an opening idea, with the lively step of a dance tune, is paralysed by the endless repetition of a narrow one-bar-phrase. The solo violin, inserting some passage work, takes the lead all through; but, as in the first movement, it does not embark upon a cadenza. So, considered from the point of view of its technical effectiveness, the Concerto has not much to offer either. In this respect too, it is very much overshadowed by Schumann's Fantasy for violin and orchestra, written not long before.

If the knowledgeable Schumannian feels emotionally affected by the second movement, a peculiar circumstance is involved. A suggestive phrase, with which the violin enters after a short orchestral prelude, turns out to be a primary, not yet fully shaped version of Schumann's last musical thought. He wrote it down on the night of 17 February 1854, ten days before his attempted suicide at the onset of his insanity, and he told Clara that it had been dictated to him by the spirits of Schubert and Mendelssohn. In the Concerto it is a short phrase of six bars, aimlessly meandering. In its final shape – it had matured in his mind, and he had obviously forgotten where it came from – it has the large breath of Schumann's finest inventions, a widely spaced, perfectly conclusive tune of twenty bars. Seven years after Schumann's death Brahms wrote a set of variations for piano duet on this melody, a deeply moving dirge for a beloved friend, dedicated to Schumann's daughter Julia.

It would be difficult to find a better exemplification of the difference between a sketchy and a fully matured invention (Ex. 30 opposite).

In this context it is worth remembering that in September 1853, shortly before Schumann started his Violin Concerto, the twenty-year-old Brahms, on Joachim's recommendation, made a visit to Düsseldorf that resulted in Schumann's last and most stupendous essay, an introduction of the young adept to the world of music proclaiming his genius, and a manifestation of enthusiasm, generosity and prophetic foresight without comparison. It was a decisive event in the life of Brahms, and perhaps the last happy experience in Schumann's life.

He never lost his youthful directness of communication, his readiness to act without restraint on the spur of the moment and with a total involvement, acting in a burst of enthusiasm. This impulsiveness makes his personality so infinitely appealing, and it is this impulsiveness that can be felt everywhere in his music. It determines both its greatness and its problems, as I have tried to explain. We may feel still more veneration for the great musician when we think of his tragic fate and the heroic struggle hidden behind his work, cut off all too early in the prime of his life.

This work was left unfinished, just like the work of Schubert, Weber, Mendelssohn, Chopin, Donizetti and Bellini – a stricken generation indeed. Considering this, the treasure of music they have left is a miracle.

Ex.30

(a) Version of the Violin Concerto

(b) Schumann's last melody

Index of Works Discussed

Cello Concerto in A minor, 57–9
Concert Allegro with Introduction, 54–5
Fantasy in C, 56
Introduction and Allegro appassionato, 54
Konzertstück in F, 55–6
Overtures
   Bride of Messina, 45–6
   Genovefa, 44–5
   Hermann & Dorothea, 47–8
   Julias Caesar, 46–7
   Manfred, 40–3
   Rhine Wine Song, 48
   Scenes from Goethe's *Faust,* 48–9
Overture, Scherzo & Finale in E major, 34–7
Piano Concerto in A minor, 49–54
Symphony No. 1 in B flat major, 14–21
Symphony No. 2 in C major, 21–3
Symphony No. 3 in E flat major, 24–8
Symphony No. 4 in D minor, 28–34
Symphony in G minor, 13
Violin Concerto in D minor, 59–63